MY NEW GOAl
IS a Better Me!!

BY Jeannette Sabatini

ISBN-13: 978-0692576816 (nettesfeathes)

ISBN-10: 0692576819

Dedication

This book is dedicated to children everywhere,
and, with love, to my husband, sons
and entire family,
who have been inspirational and supportive.

My new goal
is a better me!

I'm starting at
the count of three!

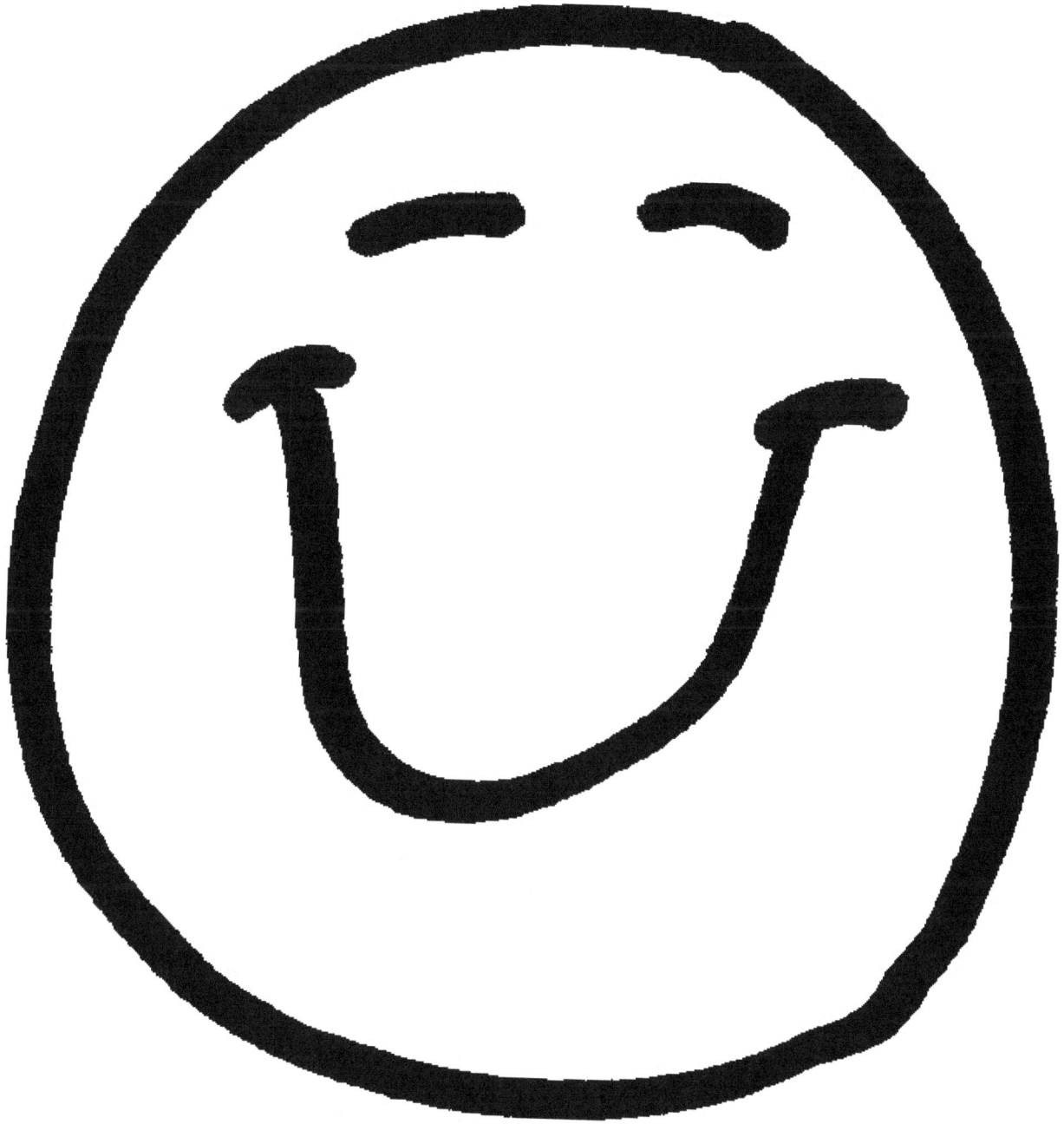

One!

Two!

Three!

I'm starting NOW!

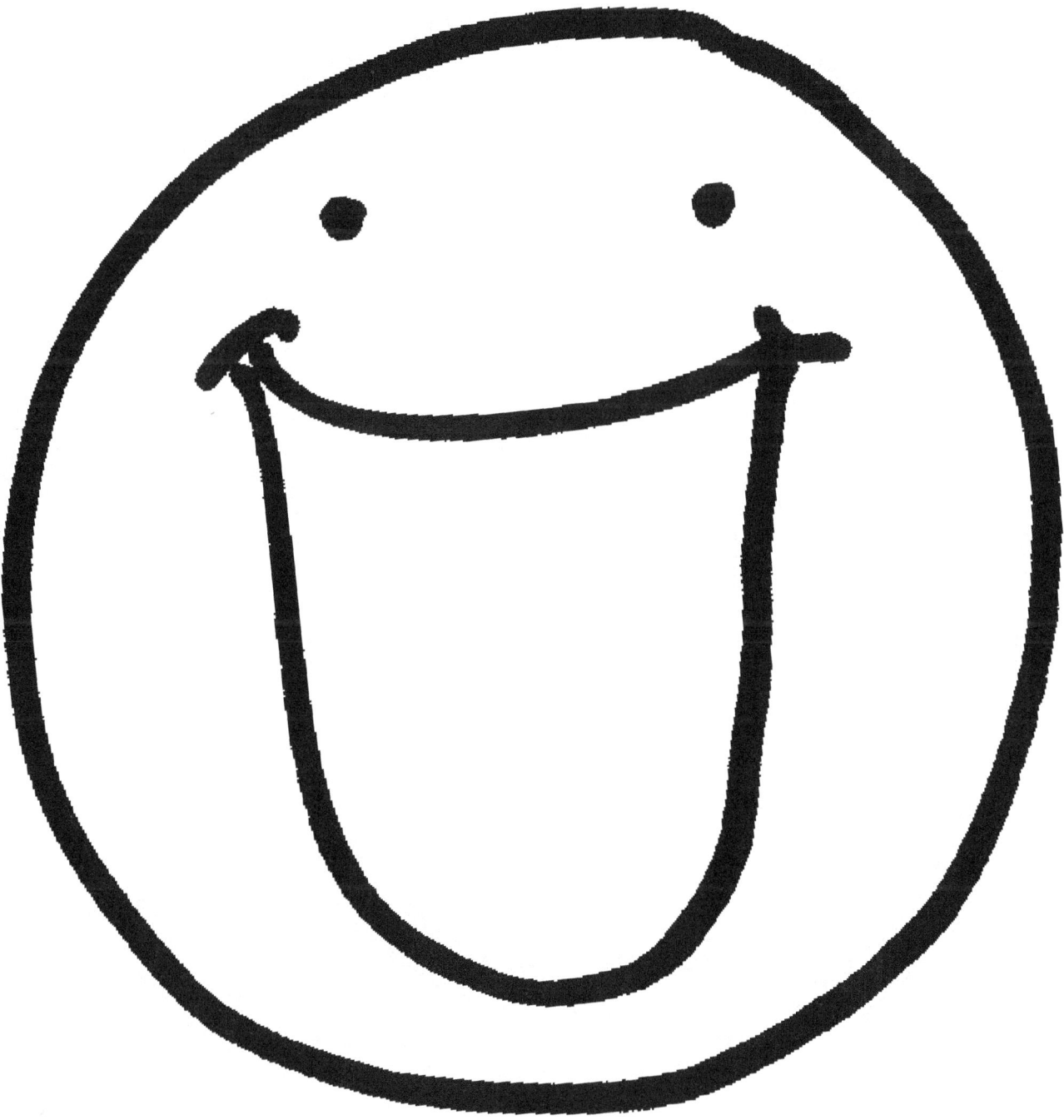

The problem is...

I don't know how!

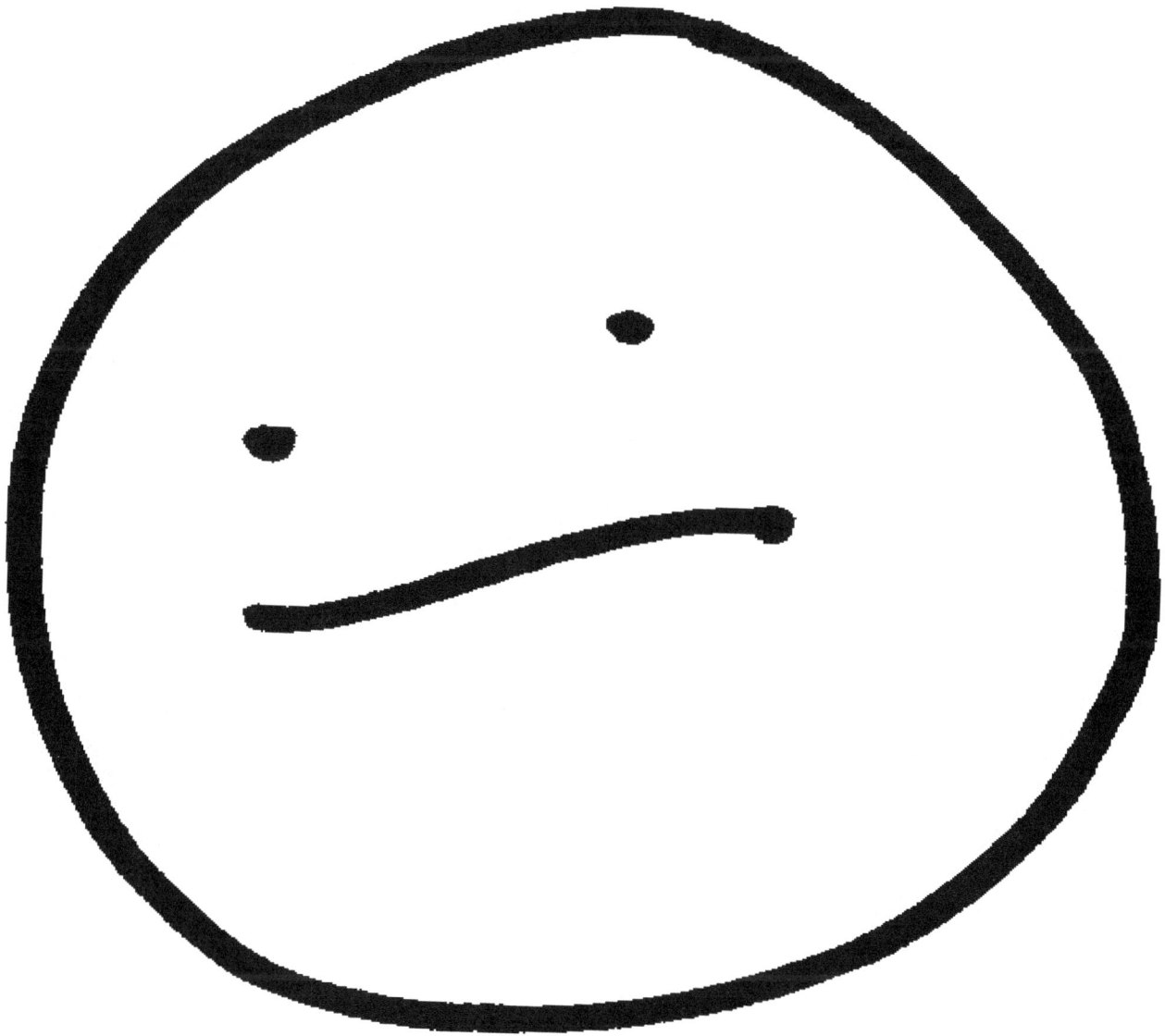

Sometimes I forget to be nice.

I've been mean... yesterday, twice!

Sometimes I point and tease.

I don't always
remember
to say
thank you or please!

I think I'll start small...
I'll start with a smile!

I'll try that, although,
it's not quite my style.

So, that's my new goal...

to smile a lot!

I think I've got it!

I'll give it a shot!

What I found was amazing!

You know what I learned?

The more smiles you give,

the more are returned!

So start small,

with a smile,

and go on from there!

My goals are

expanding...

I'm learning to care!

About "Have a Bully-Free Day!" Books

Have a Bully-Free Day! books are written to help children have a bully-free day every day at school or in the neighborhood. They build empathy and compassion and explain the rewards of being nice and the consequences of being mean. *Have a Bully-Free Day!* books help children:

- realize how negative behavior can impact friendships
- see the benefits of being friendly and positive
- welcome others into friendships
- stop seeing other kids as a threat
- deal with a person who is bullying
- be sensitive to the circumstances of others
- notice the physical signs that they have hurt another's feelings.

Kids enjoy these books because they relate to the situations presented and they enjoy the fun rhyming pattern in each. They are great for sharing: teachers can share them with a class, a counselor with a group or individual, and students with other students. Older children will enjoy acting out the skit for younger children.

The author, Jeannette Sabatini, is a writer and illustrator with a degree in English/Journalism. She has been an editor and writer in the medical field, but her experience as a mom and an elementary school aide inspired her to start writing and illustrating stories for children. She expresses her motherly advice through poetry.

This and other *Have a Bully-Free Day!* books are available on Amazon Books.

www.ingramcontent.com/pod-product-compliance
Lightning Source LLC
Chambersburg PA
CBHW081236020426
42331CB00012B/3207